Himalayan MOOD LAMP

T0364059

Running Press
Hachette Book Group
1290 Avenue of the Americas, New York, NY 10104
www.runningpress.com
@Running_Press

First Edition: October 2018

Published by Running Press, an imprint of Perseus Books, LLC, a
subsidiary of Hachette Book Group, Inc. The Running Press name
and logo is a trademark of the Hachette Book Group.

The publisher is not responsible for websites (or their content)
that are not owned by the publisher.

ISBN: 978-0-7624-6413-5

CONTENTS

Salt Rocks!

When Himalayan salt crystals formed on our planet over two hundred million years ago, minerals began making their way into the salt deposits, transforming the once pristine white salt to shades of orange and pink. Amazingly, your salt lamp is pure Himalayan rock salt and contains salt crystals that have been untouched for centuries.

Himalayan rock salt is hand-mined in the caves of northern Pakistan and a unique shape is formed. As a matter of fact, the very salt lamp you are holding is completely one of a kind, both in color and in shape—there are no two salt lamps alike. Himalayan salt lamps are most commonly a pink hue, but there are some salt lamps that can be found in white (which are rarer) or deeper shades of orange and red, depending on the rock salt's mineral content.

The Benefits of Salt Lamps

There is more than one way to reap the rewards of your salt lamp. When your lamp is turned on, you can simply gaze into the crystals and take in the tranquility of the soft, warm light. If you place your lamp in a place you frequently inhabit, such as an office, living room, bedroom, or kitchen, you will be able to get the most out of your lamp's healing powers. The benefits of pure Himalayan salt crystals are abundant, whether you choose to look at salt on a physical or spiritual level. Salt can symbolize eternity, purity, preservation, and protection. Perhaps you are familiar with the custom of throwing salt over one's shoulder to use as protection from evil?

Salt lamps are not only beautiful to look at, they are also thought to be a natural tool for protection against the harmful effects of pollution and the emittance of positive ions. People who practice Feng Shui, for example, use salt lamps for their ability to harmonize, purify, and restore their home and well-being. Himalayan salt lamps are also popularly used to purify air through their natural process of ionization, the results of which can restore the imbalances in our bodies to help us feel more energized and refreshed. For that reason it is believed by some that salt lamps can provide relief from headaches, asthma, insomnia, fatigue, anxiety, depression, and stress.

There are several relaxation techniques you can use with a salt lamp. Many people who practice meditation find that they have deeper relaxation results when they combine it with salt lamps. One such method is touching the salt lamp directly while sitting in a relaxation pose. Whether you choose to meditate with your salt lamp or simply keep it nearby, you might just discover how Himalayan salt lamps can bring a positive presence to your mental and physical space.

Air Purification and Negative Ions

You might still be wondering how salt lamps can purify the air in your living space. When the lamps are heated by the lightbulb inside, the magic of salt lamps will occur by producing and emitting a steady stream of negative ions into the air.

Researchers have demonstrated that environments with lots of negative ions can rebalance our body's vital systems while slowing down certain health problems, and can even have a positive impact on living organisms and human behavior. An environment rich in positive ions can have the opposite effect, however. Even when modern appliances such as televisions, phones, computers, microwaves, and dishwashers are not turned on, they can still emit waves of positive ions. The overbalance of positive ions is what can trigger headaches, asthma, insomnia, and other such ailments. It is no wonder why indoor spaces are the most common breeding grounds for positive ions.

So how does your salt lamp pump out negative ions into a room? To put it simply, when your salt lamp is turned on and generates enough heat, it will attract water molecules from the surrounding air and then absorb the water molecules into salt crystals. During this process, negative ions are emitted into the air, which in effect neutralizes the abundance of harmful positive ions in a room. A room with higher humidity, for instance, can greatly benefit from salt lamps.

Your Himalayan Mood Lamp

When salt lamps are glowing with the calming light they produce, they are thought to provide us with chromotherapeutic benefits. Or in other words, color therapy. This miniature lamp of yours is extra special, because unlike traditional salt lamps that only give off an orange glow, this lamp rotates through a variety of spectacular and soothing colors.

The following pages will tell you what the colors in your lamp mean and how they can enhance and restore your mood as you gaze upon your lamp.

Orange

The color orange is commonly associated with fire. Orange is the color of autumn, the setting sun, and slow burning embers that give off a warm, gentle heat. When you see the color orange in your lamp, you will feel a burst of energy. Your concentration will be enhanced and you may even come up with bright new ideas that can move you forward, inspire you to take action, and give you assurance that your destiny is in your own hands.

Yellow

The color yellow is commonly
associated with the sun. However,
yellow can be easily misunderstood
as a stimulant. Rather, yellow is in
a family of colors that soothes and
calms. When you see the color yellow
in your lamp, you will feel a sense of
peace and harmony. Your ability to
think through and consider matters
carefully will come easier. You may
even feel inspired to create and give

back to the universe in a thoughtful, meaningful way.

Pink

The color pink is associated with both softness and support. When you see pink in your lamp, your feelings of anger and neglect may feel soothed and comforted. Your stress levels may feel alleviated. Meanwhile, you can be awakened with feelings of love, compassion, and purity.

Purple

The color purple is associated with spirituality and wisdom. When you see purple in your lamp, a dream may be stimulated—whether it is a dream that cannot let go of you or one that has been a deep desire. The reminder of this dream will be a turning point for you. It may feel like a door has been opened and new possibilities are on the horizon. This will be an emotional release for you.

Blue

The color blue is commonly
associated with water, a calming force
that can heal and provide comfort.
When you see blue in your lamp, a
profound calmness will wash over you,
bringing with it deep inner peace. You
will feel that important changes are in
need of being made. Fortunately, this
restorative energy will give you clarity
and strength as you begin to face
important decisions.

Green

The color green is commonly associated with nature and earth. It is the color of balance, prosperity, curiosity, and new beginnings. When you see green in your lamp, you will feel a sense of calm and tranquility. You will be able to see things for what they truly are and discover the heart of what may be holding you back from obtaining a true balance of healthy living.

Red

The color red is commonly associated with blood, a vital element that flows through life. Without it, existence would not be possible. Red is also the color of love, passion, and desire. When you see red in your lamp, you may feel a wave of carnality. However, do not be alarmed. With the passing of such burning emotions is the replaced state of recovery, renewal, and resistance. You will soon feel reenergized and ready to take on the world stronger than you were able to before.

This book has been bound using handcraft methods and Smyth-sewn to ensure durability.

Written by Marlo Scrimizzi.

Illustrated by Anisa Makhoul.

Designed by Amanda Richmond.